W9-AWM-737

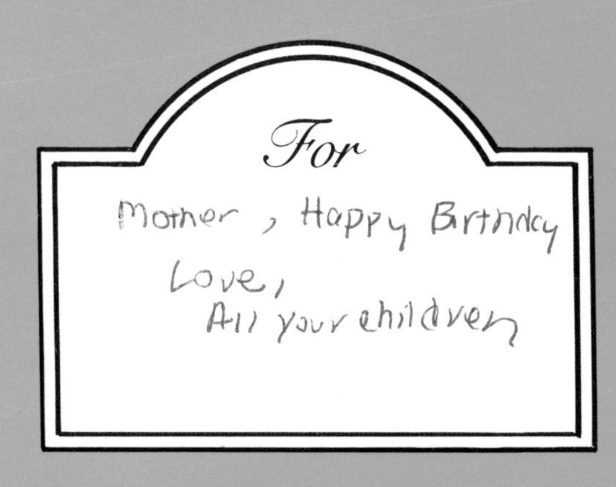
For
Mother, Happy Birthday
Love,
All your children

TO MOTHER

Edited by

LOUISE BACHELDER

PETER PAUPER PRESS, INC.
WHITE PLAINS • NEW YORK

Peter Pauper Press, Inc.
202 Mamaroneck Avenue
White Plains, NY 10601
ISBN 0-88088-540-8
Printed in Hong Kong
12 11 10

To My Dear Mother

In blessed remembrance of things past,
I dedicate this volume.

L. B.

A MOTHER's arms are made of tenderness and children sleep soundly in them.

VICTOR HUGO

WHEN God thought of MOTHER, he must have laughed with satisfaction, and framed it quickly, – so rich, so deep, so divine, so full of soul, power, and beauty, was the conception.

HENRY WARD BEECHER

ALL that I am or hope to be I owe to my angel mother. . . . I remember my mother's prayers and they have always followed me. They have clung to me all my life.

ABRAHAM LINCOLN

WHO can find a virtuous woman? for her price is far above rubies.

The heart of her husband doth safely trust in her, so that he shall have not need of spoil.

She will do him good and not evil all the days of her life.

She stretcheth out her hand to the poor; yea, she reacheth forth her hands to the needy.

Strength and honor are her clothing; and she shall rejoice in time to come.

She openeth her mouth with wisdom; and in her tongue is the law of kindness.

She looketh well to the ways of her household, and eateth not the bread of idleness.

Her children arise up, and call her blessed; her husband also, and he praiseth her.

PROVERBS 31:10-12, 19, 25-28

IN the man whose childhood has known caresses, there is always a fibre of memory that can be touched to gentle issues.

GEORGE ELIOT

My mother was the most beautiful woman I ever saw. . . . All I am I owe to my mother. . . . I attribute all my success in life to the moral, intellectual, and physical education I received from her.

George Washington

There was a place in childhood, that I
remember well,
And there a voice of sweetest tone, bright
fairy tales did tell,
And gentle words, and fond embrace, were
given with joy to me,
When I was in that happy place upon my
mother's knee.

Samuel Lover

Every man, for the sake of the great blessed Mother in Heaven, and for the love of his own little mother on earth, should handle all womankind gently, and hold them in all honor.

Alfred, Lord Tennyson

Backward, turn backward, O time, in your
flight,
Make me a child again just for to-night!
Mother, come back from the echoless shore,
Take me again to your heart as of yore;
Kiss from my forehead the furrows of care,
Smooth the few silver threads out of my hair;
Over my slumbers your loving watch keep;—
Rock me to sleep Mother — rock me to sleep!

. . . . .

Over my heart, in the days that are flown,
No love like mother-love ever has shone;
No other worship abides and endures —
Faithful, unselfish, and patient like yours:
None like a mother can charm away pain,
Long I to-night for your presence again.
Come from the silence so long and so deep; —
Rock me to sleep, Mother — rock me to sleep!

Elizabeth Akers Allen

My mother was the source from which I derived the guiding principles of my life.

John Wesley

THE mother loves her child most divinely, not when she surrounds him with comfort and anticipates his wants, but when she resolutely holds him to the highest standards and is content with nothing less than his best. . . . Happy is the child to whom the love of a mother is a noble stimulus.

HAMILTON WRIGHT MABIE

I HAD a Mother who read me lays
Of ancient and gallant and golden days;
Stories of Marmion and Ivanhoe,
Which every boy has a right to know.

I had a Mother who read me things
That wholesome life to the boy heart brings—
Stories that stir with an upward touch,
Oh, that each mother of boys were such!

You may have tangible wealth untold;
Caskets of jewels and coffers of gold.
Richer than I you can never be —
I had a Mother who read to me.

STRICKLAND GILLILAN

A MOTHER is the truest friend we have, when trials, heavy and sudden, fall upon us; when adversity takes the place of prosperity; when friends who rejoice with us in our sunshine, desert us when troubles thicken around us, still will she cling to us, and endeavor by her kind precepts and counsels to dissipate the clouds of darkness, and cause peace to return to our hearts. . . . But a mother's love endures through all; in good repute, in bad repute, in the face of the world's condemnation, a mother still loves on, and still hopes that her child may turn from his evil ways, and repent; still she remembers the infant smiles that once filled her bosom with rapture, the merry laugh, the joyful shout of his childhood, the opening promise of his youth; and she can never be brought to think him all unworthy.

WASHINGTON IRVING

CHILDHOOD is like a mirror, which reflects in after life the images first presented to it.

SAMUEL SMILES

I GAZE on the moon as I tread the drear wild,
And feel that my mother now thinks of her
child,
As she looks on that moon from our own
cottage door
Thro' the woodbine, whose fragrance shall
cheer me no more.
Home, home, sweet, sweet home!
There's no place like home, oh, there's no
place like home.

. . . .

To thee I'll return, overburdened with care;
The heart's dearest solace will smile on me
there;
No more from that cottage again will I roam;
Be it ever so humble, there's no place like
home.
Home, home, sweet, sweet home!
There's no place like home, oh, there's no
place like home.

JOHN HOWARD PAYNE

A KISS from my mother made me a painter.

BENJAMIN WEST

You painted no Madonnas
  On chapel walls in Rome;
But with a touch diviner
  You lived one in your home.
You wrote no lofty poems
  That critics counted art;
But with a nobler vision,
  You lived them in your heart.

You carved no shapeless marble
  To some high soul design
But with a finer sculpture
  You shaped this soul of mine.
You built no great cathedrals
  That centuries applaud;
But with a grace exquisite
  Your life cathedraled God.
Had I the gift of Raphael
  Or Michelangelo
O what a rare Madonna
  My mother's life would show.

THOMAS FESSENDEN

In all my efforts to learn to read, my mother shared fully my ambition and sympathized with me and aided me in every way she could. If I have done anything in life worth attention, I feel sure that I inherited the disposition from my mother.

Booker T. Washington

I thought a child was given to sanctify
A woman, set her in the sight of all
The clear-eyed heavens, a chosen minister
To do their business, and lead spirits up
The difficult blue heights. A woman lives
Not bettered, quickened toward the truth
and good
Through being a mother? – then she's none.

Elizabeth Barrett Browning

O, wondrous power! how little understood,
Entrusted to the mother's mind alone,
To fashion genius, form the soul for good,
Inspire a West, or train a Washington.

Sarah Josepha Hale

My mother had a slender, small body, but a large heart – a heart so large that everybody's grief and everybody's joys found welcome in it, and hospitable accommodation. The greatest difference which I find between her and the rest of the people whom I have known, is this, and it is a remarkable one: those others felt a strong interest in a few things, whereas to the very day of her death, she felt a strong interest in the whole world and everything and everybody in it. In all her life she never knew such a thing as a half-hearted interest in affairs and people, or an interest which drew a line and left out certain affairs and was indifferent to certain people. The invalid who takes a strenuous and indestructible interest in everything and everybody but himself, and to whom a dull moment is an unknown thing and an impossibility, is a formidable adversary for disease and a hard invalid to vanquish. I am certain that it was this feature of my mother's make-up that carried her as far toward ninety. . . .

a mighty age, a well-contested fight for life for one who at forty was so delicate of body as to be accounted a confirmed invalid and destined to pass soon away. . . . Her interest in people and animals was warm, personal, friendly. She always found something to excuse, and as a rule to love, in the toughest of them – even if she had to put it there herself. She was the natural ally and friend of the friendless.

MARK TWAIN

IF you wanted to gather up all tender memories, all lights and shadows of the heart, all banquetings and reunions, all filial, fraternal, paternal, conjugal affections, and had only just four letters with which to spell out the height and depth and length and breadth and magnitude and eternity of meaning, you would write it out with these four capital letters: HOME.

T. DE WITT TALMAGE

MY mother's chastening love I own.

JOHN GREENLEAF WHITTIER

I WAS between three and four years of age when our mother died, and my own personal recollections of her are therefore but few. But the deep interest and veneration that she inspired in all who knew her was such that, during my childhood, I was constantly hearing her spoken of, and, from one friend or another, some incident or anecdote of her life was constantly being impressed on me.

Mother was one of those strong, restful, yet widely sympathetic natures, in whom all around seemed to find comfort and repose.

Although mother's bodily presence disappeared from our circle, I think that her memory and example had more influence in molding her family, in deterring from evil and exciting to good, than the living presence of many mothers. It was a memory that met us everywhere, for every person in town, from the highest to the lowest, seemed to have been so impressed by her character and life that they constantly reflected some portion of it back on us.

HARRIET BEECHER STOWE

My mother was as mild as any saint,
And nearly canonized by all she knew,
So gracious was her tact and tenderness.

ALFRED, LORD TENNYSON

THERE is none,
In all this cold and hollow world, no fount
Of deep, strong, deathless love, save that
within
A mother's heart.

FELICIA HEMANS

AND say to mothers what a holy charge
Is theirs – with what a kingly power their
love
Might rule the fountains of the new-born
mind.

LYDIA HUNTLY SIGOURNEY

YEARS to a mother bring distress
But do not make her love the less.

WILLIAM WORDSWORTH

CHILDREN are what the mothers are.

WALTER SAVAGE LANDOR

THE future destiny of the child is always the work of the mother.

NAPOLEON

MANY make the household but only one the home.

JAMES RUSSELL LOWELL

HOMES are for mothers as nests are for birds.

ARTHUR B. LAUGHLIN

No joy in nature is so sublimely affecting as the joy of a mother at the good fortune of her child.

JEAN PAUL RICHTER

HEAVEN lies about us in our infancy.

ALPHONSE M. L. LAMARTINE

THOU, while thy babes around thee cling,
Shalt show us how divine a thing
A woman may be made.

WILLIAM WORDSWORTH

The woman who creates and sustains a home, and under whose hands children grow up to be strong and pure men and women is a creator second only to God.

Helen Hunt Jackson

All mothers are rich when they love their children.
There are no poor mothers, no ugly ones, no old ones.
Their love is always the most beautiful of the joys.
And when they seem most sad, it needs but a kiss which they receive or give to turn all their tears into stars in the depth of their eyes.

Maurice Maeterlinck

At first babes feed on the mother's bosom, but always on her heart.

Henry Ward Beecher

The mother's heart is the child's schoolroom.

Henry Ward Beecher

THERE was a child went forth every day,
And the first object he look'd upon that
object he became,
And that object became part of him for the
day or a certain part of the day,
Or for many years or stretching cycles of
years.

. . . . .

His own parents, he that had father'd him and
she that had conceiv'd him in her womb
and birth'd him,
They gave this child more of themselves than
that,
They gave him afterward every day, they
became part of him.
The mother at home quietly placing the
dishes on the supper-table,
The mother with mild words, clean her cap
and gown, a wholesome odor falling off
her person and clothes as she walks by, . . .
The family usages, the language, the com-
pany, the furniture, the yearning and
swelling heart,

Affection that will not be gainsay'd, the
sense of what is real, the thought if after
all it should prove unreal,
The doubts of daytime and the doubts of
night-time, the curious whether and how,
Whether that which appears so is so, or is it
all flashes and specks?

. . . . .

These became part of that child who went
forth every day, and now goes, and will
always go forth every day.

WALT WHITMAN

SEE how a mother, the best philosopher in practical matters, understands every one of her children and the special differences between them all; and does she not carry herself with true intuition as to their daily needs and with the interpreting philosophy of sensitive love? She is the best trainer of men and has the best mental philosophy, so far as practical things are concerned.

HENRY WARD BEECHER

CHILDREN, look into those eyes, listen to the dear voice, notice the feeling of even a single touch that is bestowed upon you by that gentle hand! Make much of it while yet you have that most precious of all good gifts, – a loving mother. Read the unfathomable love of those eyes; the kind anxiety of that tone and look, however slight your pain. In after life you may have friends, fond, dear friends, but never will you have again the inexpressible love and gentleness lavished upon you, which none but mother bestows.

THOMAS BABINGTON MACAULAY

HUNDREDS of stars in the pretty sky,
Hundreds of shells on the shore together,
Hundreds of birds that go singing by,
Hundreds of birds in the sunny weather,
Hundreds of dewdrops to greet the dawn,
Hundreds of bees in the purple clover,
Hundreds of butterflies on the lawn,
But only *one mother* the wide world over.

GEORGE COOPER

WHAT matter how the night behaved?
What matter how the north-wind raved?
Blow high, blow low, not all its snow
Could quench our hearth-fire's ruddy glow.

. . . . .

And while with care our mother laid
The work aside, her steps she stayed
One moment, seeking to express
Her grateful sense of happiness
For food and shelter, warmth and health,
And love's contentment more than wealth,
With simple wishes (not the weak,
Vain prayers which no fulfillment seek,
But such as warm the generous heart
O'er-prompt to do with Heaven its part)
That none might lack, that bitter night,
For bread and clothing, warmth and light.

JOHN GREENLEAF WHITTIER

SIT with me at the homestead hearth,
And stretch the hands of memory forth
To warm them at the wood-fire's blaze.

JOHN GREENLEAF WHITTIER

A HEALTHY home, presided over by a thrifty, cleanly woman, is the abode of comfort, of virtue, and of happiness. It is the scene of every ennobling relation in family life. It is endeared to a man by many delightful memories, by the affectionate voices of his wife, his children, and his neighbors. Such a home is regarded . . . as a training ground for young immortals, a sanctuary for the heart, a refuge from storm, a sweet resting place after labor, a consolation in sorrow, a pride in success, and a joy at all times.

SAMUEL SMILES

HER ample gown is of cream-hued linen:
Her grandsons raised the flax and her grand-
daughters spun it with the distaff and
wheel.
The melodious character of the earth,
The finish beyond which philosophy cannot
go, and does not wish to go,
The justified mother of men.

WALT WHITMAN

THE loss of a mother is always felt; even though her health may incapacitate her from taking any active part in the care of the family, still she is a sweet rallying point, around which affection and obedience and a thousand tender endeavors to please, concentrate; and – dreary is the blank when such a point is withdrawn.

ALPHONSE M. L. LAMARTINE

THEY tell us of an Indian tree
Which howsoe'er the sun and sky
May tempt its boughs to wander free,
And shoot and blossom, wide and high,
Far better loves to bend its arms
Downward again to that dear earth
From which the life, that fills and warms
Its grateful being, first had birth.
'Tis thus, though wooed by flattering friends,
And fed with fame (if fame it be),
This heart, my own dear mother, bends,
With love's true instinct back to thee!

THOMAS MOORE

MOTHER – that was the bank where we deposited all our hurts and worries.

T. DEWITT TALMAGE

BECAUSE I feel that, in the Heavens above,
The angels, whispering to one another,
Can find, among their burning terms of love,
None so devotional as that of "Mother,"
Therefore by that dear name I long have called you –
You who are more than mother unto me,
And fill my heart of hearts, where Death installed you,
In setting my Virginia's spirit free.
My mother – my own mother, who died early,
Was but the mother of myself; but you
Are mother to the one I loved so dearly,
And thus are dearer than the mother I knew
By that infinity with which my wife
Was dearer to my soul than its soul-life.

EDGAR ALLAN POE

MY MOTHER's influence in molding my character was conspicuous. She forced me to learn daily long chapters of the Bible by heart. To that discipline and patient, accurate resolve I owe not only much of my general power of taking pains, but the best part of my taste for literature.

JOHN RUSKIN

THEY say that man is mighty;
He governs land and sea,
He wields a mighty scepter
O'er lesser powers that be.
But a mightier power and stronger
Man from his throne has hurled,
For the hand that rocks the cradle
Is the hand that rules the world.

WILLIAM ROSS WALLACE

WHERE there is a mother in the house, matters speed well.

AMOS BRONSON ALCOTT

So many memories of the past present themselves when one tries to revive in fancy the features of a beloved being, that one views them dimly through these memories, as through tears. These are the tears of imagination. When I try to recall my mother as she was at that time, nothing appears to me but her brown eyes, which always expressed love and goodness; the mole on her neck a little lower down than the spot where the short hairs grow; her white embroidered collar; her cool, soft hand, which petted me so often, and which I so often kissed: but her image as a whole escapes me.

. . . . .

Beautiful as seemed mamma's face, it became incomparably more lovely when she smiled, and seemed to enliven everything about her. If in life's trying moments I could catch but a glimpse of that smile, I should not know what grief is. It seems to me that what is called beauty of face consists in the smile alone: if the smile adds charm to the face,

then the face is very fine; if it does not alter the countenance, then the latter is ordinary; if it spoils it, then it is bad.

LEO TOLSTOI

MY Blessed Mother dozing in her chair
On Christmas Day seemed an embodied
  Love,
A comfortable Love with soft brown hair
Softened and silvered to a tint of dove;
A better sort of Venus with an air
Angelical from thoughts that dwell above;
A wiser Pallas in whose body fair
Enshrined a blessed soul looks out thereof.
Winter brought holly then; now Spring has
  brought
Paler and frailer snowdrops shivering;
And I have brought a simple humble
  thought –
I her devoted duteous Valentine –
A lifelong thought which drills this song
  I sing.
A lifelong love to this dear saint of mine.

CHRISTINA G. ROSSETTI

Do you not suppose that love has anger? Do you suppose that when a mother sees the child that is both herself and him doing a detestable meanness, that she is not angry, that the child does not feel the smart of physical advice? I tell you that there is no such indignation possible as the indignation that means rescue, help, hope, and betterment. Has love no specialty or discrimination in removing error – nor any continuing, intense regard for specific and exact truth? God has it and we are like him. We are his children, and know it by that. Love is simply that which overhangs all these powers, which gives them quality and direction.

HENRY WARD BEECHER

MOST of all the other beautiful things in life come by twos and threes, by dozens and hundreds. Plenty of roses, stars, sunsets, rainbows, brothers and sisters, aunts and cousins, but only one *mother* in the whole world.

KATE DOUGLAS WIGGIN

WE never know the love of the parent till we become parents ourselves. When we first bend over the cradle of our own child, God throws back the temple door, and reveals to us the sacredness and mystery of the father's and mother's love to ourselves. And in later years, when they have gone from us, there is always a certain sorrow, that we cannot tell them we have found it out. One of the deepest experiences of a noble nature in reference to the loved ones that have passed beyond this world is the thought of what he might have been to them if he had known while they were living, what he has learned since they died.

HENRY WARD BEECHER

THE Spartan spirit that made life so grand,
Mating poor daily needs
With high, heroic deeds,
That wrested happiness from Fate's hard
hand.

LOUISA MAY ALCOTT

SHE broke the bread into two fragments and gave them to the children, who ate with avidity.

"She hath kept none for herself," grumbled the Sergeant.

"Because she is not hungry," said a soldier.

"Because she is a mother," said the Sergeant.

VICTOR HUGO

I NOW plainly perceive what great obligations I am under to love and honour my parents. I have great reason to believe that their counsel and education have been my making; though, in the time of it, it seemed to do me so little good. I have reason to hope that their prayers for me have been, in many things, very powerful and prevalent, that God has, in many things, taken me under his care and guidance, provision and direction, in answer to their prayers for me. I was never so sensible of it as now.

JONATHAN EDWARDS

OBSERVE how soon, and to what a degree, this influence begins to operate! Her first ministration for her infant is to enter, as it were, the valley of the shadow of death, and win its life at the peril of her own! How different must an affection thus founded be from all others.

LYDIA HUNTLEY SIGOURNEY

A PICTURE memory brings to me:
I look across the year and see
Myself beside my mother's knee.

I feel her gentle hand restrain
My selfish moods, and know again
A child's blind sense of wrong and pain.

But wiser now, a man gray grown,
My childhood's needs are better known,
My mother's chastening love I own.

JOHN GREENLEAF WHITTIER

WHERE yet was ever found a mother
Who'd give her booby for another?

JOHN GAY

My mother was an angel upon earth. She was a minister of blessing to all human beings within her sphere of action. . . . She had no feelings but of kindness and beneficence, yet her mind was as firm as her temper was mild and gentle. She had known sorrow, but her sorrow was silent. . . . She had been fifty years the delight of my father's heart. If there is existence and retribution beyond the grave, my mother is happy. But if virtue alone is happiness below, never was existence upon earth more blessed than hers.

John Quincy Adams

I would desire for a friend the son who never resisted the tears of his mother.

Lacretalle

From father have I my stature
My zest for earnest living,
From little mother my gay nature
My love of story-telling.

Johann Wolfgang von Goethe

THEN spake the woman, whose the living child was, unto the king, for her bowels yearned upon her son, and she said, O my lord, give her the living child, and in no wise slay it. But the other said, Let it be neither mine nor thine; but divide it.

Then the king answered and said, Give her the living child, and in no wise slay it: she is the mother thereof.

I KINGS 3:26, 27

WHATEVER brawls disturb the street,
There should be peace at home.

ISAAC WATTS

SUBDUING and subdued, the petty strife,
Which clouds the colour of domestic life;
The sober comfort, all the peace which
springs
From the large aggregate of little things;
On these small cares of daughter, wife or
friend,
The almost sacred joys of home depend.

HANNAH MORE

In general those parents have the most reverence who deserve it.

SAMUEL JOHNSON

Happy is he that is happy in his children.

THOMAS FULLER

If I had but two little wings
And were a little feathery bird,
To you I'd fly, my dear!
But thoughts like these are idle things,
And I stay here.

But in my sleep to you I fly:
I'm always with you in my sleep!
The world is all one's own.
But then one wakes, and where am I?
All, all alone.

Sleep stays not, though a monarch bids:
So I love to wake ere break of day:
For though my sleep be gone,
Yet while 'tis dark, one shuts one's lids,
And still dreams on.

SAMUEL TAYLOR COLERIDGE

WHAT are Raphael's Madonnas but the shadow of a mother's love, fixed in permanent outline forever?

THOMAS WENTWORTH HIGGINSON

HIS sweetest dreams were still of that dear voice that soothed his infancy.

ROBERT SOUTHEY

LONG years you've kept the door ajar
To greet me, coming from afar:
Long years in my accustomed place
I've read my welcome in your face,
And felt the sunlight of your love
Drive back the years and gently move
The telltale shadow 'round to youth,
You've found the very spring, in truth,
That baffles time – the kindly joy
That keeps me in your heart a boy,
And now I send an unknown guest
To bide with you and snugly rest
Beside the old home's ingle-nook. –
For love of me you'll love my book.

ROBERT BRIDGES

MOTHERS are the only goddesses in whom the whole world believes.

ANONYMOUS

DON'T poets know
Better than others?
God can't be always everywhere: and, so,
Invented Mothers.

SIR EDWIN ARNOLD

FOR me, a line from my mother is more efficacious than all the homilies preached in Lent.

HENRY WADSWORTH LONGFELLOW

A LADY, the loveliest ever the sun
Looked down upon you must paint for me;
O, if I only could make you see
The clear blue eyes, the tender smile,
The sovereign sweetness, the gentle grace,
The woman's soul, and the angel's face
That are beaming on me all this while,
I need not speak these foolish words:
Yet one word tells you all I would say, —
She is my mother.

ALICE CARY

WHEREVER a true wife goes, home is always round her. Only the stars may be over her head; the glowworm in the night-cold grass may be the only fire at her foot; but home is yet wherever she is; and, for a noble woman, it stretches far 'round her, better than ceiled with cedar, or painted with vermilion, shedding its quiet light far, for those who else were homeless.

JOHN RUSKIN

CAN a mother sit and hear
An infant groan, an infant fear?
No, no! never can it be!
Never, never can it be!

WILLIAM BLAKE

"SHE made home happy!" these few words
I read
Within a churchyard, written on a stone;
No name, no date, the simple words alone,
Told me the story of the unknown dead.

HENRY COYLE

THERE is a religion in all deep love, but the love of a mother is the veil of a softer light between the heart and the heavenly Father.

SAMUEL TAYLOR COLERIDGE

THREE words fall sweetly on my soul,
As music from an angel's lyre,
That bid my spirit spurn control,
And upward to its source aspire;
The sweetest sounds to mortals given
Are heard in Mother, Home, and Heaven.

WILLIAM GOLDSMITH BROWN

WOMEN know
The way to rear up children (to be just)
They have a merry, simple, tender knack
Of trying sashes, fitting babies' shoes,
And stringing pretty words that make no
sense,
And kissing full sense into empty words;
Which things are corals to cut life upon
Although such trifles.

ELIZABETH BARRETT BROWNING

HOME – there is a magic in that little word, – it is a mystic circle that surrounds comforts and virtues never known beyond its hallowed limits.

ROBERT SOUTHEY

SHE seemed an angel to our infant eyes!
Once, when the glorifying moon revealed
Her who at evening by our pillow kneeled –
Soft-voiced and golden haired, from holy
skies
Flown to her loves on wings of Paradise –
We looked to see the pinions half-concealed.
The Tuscan vines and olives will not yield
Her back to me, who loved her in the wise,
And since have little known her, but have
grown
To see another mother, tenderly,
Watch over sleeping darlings of her own;
Perchance the years have changed her: yet
alone
This picture lingers: still she seems to me
The fair, young Angel of my infancy.

EDMUND CLARENCE STEDMAN

KINDNESS is contagious. The spirit of harmony trickles down by a thousand secret channels into the inmost recesses of the household life. One truly affectionate soul in a family will exert a sweetening and harmonizing influence upon all its members. It is hard to be angry in the presence of imperturbable good-nature. It is well-nigh impossible to be morose in face of a cheerful and generous helpfulness. Beginning with the highest, the ointment drops even upon those who are unconscious or careless of it, and the whole house is presently filled with its fragrance.

HENRY VAN DYKE

WHO is it that loves me and will love me forever with an affection which no chance, no misery, no crime of mine can do away? . . . My dear mother, with the truthfulness of a mother's heart, ministered to all my woes, outward and inward, and even against hope kept prophesying good.

THOMAS CARLYLE

CHILDREN have more need of models than of critics.

JOSEPH JOUBERT

SONNETS are full of love, and this my tome
Has many sonnets: so here now shall be
One sonnet more, a loving sonnet from me
To her whose heart is my heart's quiet home,
To my first Love, my Mother on whose knee
I learnt love-lore that is not troublesome:
Whose service is my special dignity
And she my lodestar while I go and come.
And so because you love, and because
I love you, Mother, I have woven a wreath
Of rhymes wherewith to crown your honored name:
In you not fourscore years can dim the flame
Of love, whose blessed glow transcends the laws
Of time and change and mortal life and death.

CHRISTINA G. ROSSETTI

In a child's lunch basket, a mother's thoughts.

Japanese Proverb

If I were hanged on the highest hill,
Mother o' mine, O mother o' mine!
I know whose love would follow me still,
Mother o' mine, O mother o' mine!
If I were drowned in the deepest sea,
Mother o' mine, O mother o' mine!
I know whose tears would come down to me,
Mother o' mine, O mother o' mine!
If I were damned by body and soul,
I know whose prayers would make me
whole,
Mother o' mine, O mother o' mine!

Rudyard Kipling

This fond attachment to the well-known
place
When first we started into life's long race,
Maintains its hold with such unfailing sway,
We feel it e'en in age, and at our latest day.

William Cowper

TRAIN up a child in the way he should go;
and when he is old, he will not depart from it.

PROVERBS 22:6

A MOTHER's love is the golden link
Binding youth to age;
And he is still but a child,
However time may have furrowed his cheek,
Who cannot happily recall, with a softened
heart,
The fond devotion and gentle chidings
Of the best friend God ever gave.

CHRISTIAN BOVÉE

A WOMAN's love
Is mighty, but a mother's heart is weak,
And by its weakness overcomes.

JAMES RUSSELL LOWELL

THE Crown of the Home is Godliness;
The Beauty of the Home is Order;
The Glory of the Home is Hospitality;
The Blessing of the Home is Contentment.

HENRY VAN DYKE

EUGENE Field's mother was a handsome woman, possessed of great strength of character, which was accompanied by rare sweetness and gentleness. Although only a boy of six when he lost his mother, he said in later years, "I have carried the remembrance of her gentle voice and soothing touch all through my life."

IDA COMSTOCK BELOW

THERE is no love like the good old love – the love that mother gave us.

EUGENE FIELD

THE world has no flower in any land,
And no such pearl in any gulf or sea,
As any babe on any mother's knee.

ALGERNON CHARLES SWINBURNE

MOTHER love . . . hath this unlikeness to any other love: Tender to the object, it can be infinitely tyrannical to itself, and thence all its power of self-sacrifice.

LEW WALLACE

OUR mother bade us keep the trodden ways,
Stroked down my tippet, set my brother's
frill,
Then with the benediction of her gaze,
Clung to us lessening and pursued us still
Across the homestead to the rookery elms
Whose tall old trunks had each a grassy
mound,
So rich for us, we counted them as realms
With varied products; here were earth nuts
found
And here the Lady-fingers, in deep shade,
Here sloping toward the moat the rushes
grew,
The large to split for pith, the small to braid
While over all the dark rooks cawing flew –
And made a happy strange solemnity
A deep-toned chant from life unknown to
me.

GEORGE ELIOT

MOTHER's love grows by giving.

CHARLES LAMB

I value this delicious home feeling as one of the choicest gifts a parent can bestow.

Washington Irving

Unhappy is the man for whom his own mother has not made all other mothers venerable.

Jean Paul Richter

Love droops; youth fades;
The leaves of friendship fall;
A mother's love outlives them all.

Oliver Wendell Holmes

Mother is the name for God in the lips and hearts of little children.

William Makepeace Thackeray

Who ran to help me when I fell,
And would some pretty story tell,
Or kiss the place to make it well?
My mother.

Jane Taylor

A MOTHER has, perhaps, the hardest earthly lot; and yet no mother worthy of the name ever gave herself thoroughly for her child who did not feel that, after all, she reaped what she had sown.

HENRY WARD BEECHER

YET was there one . . .
Not learned, save in gracious household
ways,
Not perfect, nay, but full of tender wants,
No Angel, but a dearer being, all dipped
In Angel instincts, breathing Paradise,
Interpreter between the Gods and men,
Who looked all native to her place . . .
Happy he
With such a mother! faith in womankind
Beats with his blood, and trust in all things
high
Comes easy to him, and though he trip and
fall
He shall not blind his soul with clay.

ALFRED, LORD TENNYSON

ALL-GRACIOUS! grant to those who bear
A mother's charge, the strength and light
To guide the feet that own their care
In ways of Love and Truth and Right.

WILLIAM CULLEN BRYANT

THE poor wren,
The most diminutive of birds, will fight
The young ones in her nest against the owl.

WILLIAM SHAKESPEARE

As years ago we carried to your knees
The tales and treasures of eventful days,
Knowing no deed too humble for your
praise,
Nor any gift too trivial to please,
So still we bring, with older smiles and tears,
What gifts we may, to claim the old, dear
right;
Your faith, beyond the silence and the night,
Your love still close and watching through
the years.

KATHLEEN NORRIS

If the whole world were put into one scale, and my mother in the other, the whole world would kick the beam.

Lord Langdale

Home's not merely four square walls,
Though with pictures hung and gilded;
Home is where Affection calls –
Filled with shrines the Hearth had builded!
Home! Go watch the faithful dove,
Sailing 'neath the heaven above us.
Home is where there's one to love!
Home is where there's one to love us.

Home's not merely roof and room,
It needs something to endear it;
Home is where the heart can bloom,
Where there's some kind lip to cheer it!
What is home with none to meet,
None to welcome, none to greet us?
Home is sweet, and only sweet,
Where there's one we love to meet us!

Charles Swain

Is not a young mother one of the sweetest sights which life shows us?

WILLIAM MAKEPEACE THACKERAY

ONLY a mother's heart can be
Patient enough for such as he. . . .

ETHEL LYNN BEERS

As pure and sweet, her fair brow seemed
eternal as the sky;
And like the brook's low song, her voice, a
sound which could not die.
Sweet promptings unto kindest deeds were
in her very look;
We read her face, as one who reads a true
and holy book.

JOHN GREENLEAF WHITTIER

A HOUSE is built of logs and stone,
Of tiles and posts and piers,
A home is built of loving deeds
That stand a thousand years.

VICTOR HUGO

THE light upon his eyelids pricked them wide
And staring out at us with all their blue,
As half perplexed between the angelhood
He had been away to visit in his sleep,
And our most mortal presence, gradually
He saw his mother's face, accepting it
In change for heaven itself with such a smile
As might have well been learnt there.

ELIZABETH BARRETT BROWNING

LORD, who ordainest for mankind
Benignant toils and tender cares!
We thank Thee for the ties that bind
The mother to the child she bears.

WILLIAM CULLEN BRYANT

WHATSO gifts the years bestow,
Still men know,
While breathes, lives one who sees
(Stand they pure or sin-defiled)
But the child
Whom she crooned to sleep and rocked
upon her knee.

EMMA LAZARUS

THE greatest battle that ever was fought –
  Shall I tell you where and when?
On the maps of the world you will find it not:
  It was fought by the Mothers of Men.

Not with cannon or battle shot,
  With sword or nobler pen;
Not with eloquent word or thought
  From the wonderful minds of men;

But deep in a walled-up woman's heart;
  A woman that would not yield;
But bravely and patiently bore her part;
  Lo! there is the battlefield.

No marshalling troops, no bivouac song,
  No banner to gleam and wave;
But, Oh, these battles they last so long –
  From babyhood to the grave!

But faithful still as a bridge of stars
  She fights in her walled-up town;
Fights on and on in the endless wars;
  Then silent, unseen goes down!

Ho! ye with banners and battle shot,
With soldiers to shout and praise,
I tell you the kingliest victories fought
Are fought in these silent ways.

JOAQUIN MILLER

MY mother she's so good to me, if I was good as I could be, I couldn't be as good, no, sir; can't any boy be good as her.

JAMES WHITCOMB RILEY

THE bearing and the training of a child is woman's wisdom.

ALFRED, LORD TENNYSON

I MISS thee, my Mother! Thy image is still
The deepest impressed on my heart.

ELIZA COOK

HONOR thy father and thy mother, that thy days may be long upon the land which the Lord thy God giveth thee.

EXODUS 20:12